D0729284

Something Is About To Happen ...

*Sermons For Advent
And Christmas*

Thomas G. Long

CSS Publishing Company, Inc., Lima, Ohio

SOMETHING IS ABOUT TO HAPPEN ...

Revised Edition

Some scripture quotations are from the *New Revised Standard Version of the Bible*, copyright 1989 by the Division of Christian Education of the National Council of the Churches of Christ in the USA. Used by permission.

Some scripture quotations are from the *Revised Standard Version of the Bible*, copyrighted 1946, 1952 © 1971, 1973, by the Division of Christian Education of the National Council of the Churches of Christ in the USA. Used by permission.

Library of Congress Cataloging-in-Publication Data

Long, Thomas G., 1946-

    Something is about to happen : sermons for Advent and Christmas / Thomas G. Long. — Rev. ed.
        p.   cm.
    Rev. ed. of: Shepherds and bathrobes.
    Includes bibliographical references.
    ISBN 0-7880-0866-8
    1. Advent sermons. 2. Christmas sermons. 3. Epiphany season—sermons. 4. Sermons, American. I. Long, Thomas G., 1946- Shepherds and bathrobes. II. Title.

BV40.L66   1996
252'.61—dc20   96-30408
                                                          CIP

This book is available in the following formats, listed by ISBN:
    0-7880-0866-8   Book
    0-7880-0867-6   IBM 3 1/2
    0-7880-0868-4   Mac
    0-7880-0869-2   Sermon Prep

PRINTED IN U.S.A.

To my mother and father, who,
as the best of their many gifts,
taught me the gospel.

Table Of Contents

Foreword

Playwright Herb Gardner once described a dream he keeps having. He is seated on a theater stage, frantically scribbling on a pad. On the other side of the drawn curtain can be heard the rustlings and coughings of an audience gathering. The stage manager is nervously pacing, repeatedly glancing at Gardner, who continues to write furiously. It is opening night, and the play is not finished.

Every preacher recognizes this dream and can tell his or her version of it. It is Sunday morning, the congregation settles into the pews after the final stanza of the sermon hymn, all eyes are on the pulpit, an air of electric quietness fills the sanctuary with anticipation ... and the sermon is not finished.

Whatever psychological value such preachers' dreams carry, they also point to a truth about sermons: they are *never* finished. There is always something else, something more, which can be said, should be said, but the time for preaching has arrived, and frail and incomplete thoughts must fill that deep cavern so innocently labeled "The Sermon." The broken labors of our hands and minds must now be trusted to the continuing sustenance of the Spirit and the faithful care of those who hear. This, then, is a collection of unfinished sermons. I am willing to let them go only because of the hope that, as they are read, they will become more finished in the reader's mind than they are in mine.

All of the sermons in this collection are based upon biblical texts. In every case, a serious attempt was made to listen to the text. Some of these texts were frustratingly silent, and, like Jacob wrestling the angel, I had to cling to them, begging for a blessing. Other passages were eager to speak, often saying more than I could retain and always more than I could understand.

These sermons represent a wide variety of styles and methods. This variety is a result, not of stylistic playfulness, but rather from an attempt to let the tone and substance of the texts govern the shapes of the sermons. One additional factor influenced composition. I was aware that these sermons would be *read*, rather than *heard,* and they are, therefore, written for the "eye" rather than for the "ear." Because of this, they are not, I suppose, actually sermons at all, since preaching is at home only in orality. If, however, they are read by ministers and teachers who find in them some help for their own task of announcing the good news, then I will be content in the knowledge that these sermons have found their way home.

Thomas G. Long
Princeton, New Jersey

When Something Is About To Happen

Mark 13:32-37

"I'll tell you what keeps me coming to this church." The man who spoke was punching the air with his finger, pronouncing every word with force, and the dozen or so other people in the room turned to listen. The group called themselves the "Searchers Class," and had done so since the time, more than ten years before, when, as young adults, they had formed an alternative church school class. As the "Searchers" crept into middle age, the act of searching itself seemed to take more and more energy. Indeed, the whole business of being a part of the church at all felt, at times, like a burdensome weight, and on this Sunday morning that weight had tugged the conversation toward the question: Why stay in the church?

"I'll tell you," he said, "what keeps me coming to this church," and every head turned in his direction. The sudden rush of interest made him hesitate, uncertain of his own thought, but he pushed on. "It's strange, I know, but I get the feeling here, like nowhere else, that something is about to happen."

The feeling that something is about to happen. A strange notion, and yet, the earliest Christians would have recognized it instantly as one of the truest marks of the church. They were convinced they stood on the precipice of history, and that something, indeed, was about to happen. For the world, time lumbered on, day after wearisome day, moving toward who knows what, but, for the early Christian community, something was about to happen. As time crept forward, a great, though yet unseen, future had stirred and gathered itself, and now was sweeping toward time itself on a course of inevitable collision. Something was about to happen.

What was about to happen? Their attempts to describe it strained the boundaries of their language as surely as they strain our contemporary imaginations. "The kingdom of God is at hand ... The stars will fall from heaven ... The night is far gone ... They will see the Son of man coming in clouds with great power and glory ... This age is passing away ... Come, Lord, Jesus." The church lived on tiptoe, straining their eyes toward the horizon. Something was about to happen.

Because something was about to happen, every word they uttered, every deed they did, every prayer they prayed was shaped by this coming event. Like an actor in a play whose role seems insignificant until the denouement discloses that his lines held the key to the truth all along, the early Christians risked the shame of the world, confidently awaiting the final act.

We have all known, in small ways, the energy an eagerly anticipated future can give to our actions in the present. The expectant parents who find joy in what would otherwise be toil: assembling the crib, painting the nursery, practicing the pushing and the breathing. The residents of a town who mow the lawns, sweep the sidewalks, repair the cracked windows at city hall, and stretch colorful bunting across the store fronts as they ready themselves for the visit of a dignitary. Christmas itself has this kind of power. People brave crowds at the mall and edgy clerks; gifts are carefully chosen, packages wrapped, and ceramic nativity scenes dusted and set, piece by piece, on the mantle. Every action has meaning, because something is about to happen.

But we have also known the sense of loss and disappointment over a hoped-for future which does not come, when nothing, nothing really, happens. The husband and wife who try to conceive a child, in vain. Or again, plans are changed; the dignitary travels by another route, bypassing the town, leaving the once-festive bunting to droop in the rain. Even Christmas day has its own measure of disappointment. The packages are opened, the gifts admired and put away. The tree comes down; the shepherds and angels are stored for another year, and the long-awaited day passes with a sense that nothing, nothing really, has happened.

In a far more profound way, the church has always struggled with its pain over a future which fails to come. "Come, Lord Jesus," they prayed, but it was Roman soldiers who came. "This world is passing away," they sang, but the world remained. One can live on tiptoe just so long, before the muscles grow tired and the eyes grow weary of looking for the light of a day which never dawns. If the church is standing at the threshold of God's future kingdom of justice, then the church can dare to touch the wounds of lepers and freely pour out its resources for the poor. If this world is surely in the throes of death, and the new age of healing and mercy is close at hand, then the church can cheerfully bear rejection, endure suffering, and faithfully sing its alleluias. But if there is no God-shaped future at hand, if nothing, nothing really, is about to happen, then there is only one more day to be endured in an endless string of days, a bottomless pit of human need, and a ceaseless line of the poor, who are always with us. All there is left for the church to be is another well-meaning institution, and all there is left for the church to do is to whistle its liturgy in the dark, collect the pledge cards and keep the copy machines humming. Because nothing is about to happen.

Even the second generation of Christians, the ones to whom the New Testament was originally addressed, were not immune to this loss of faith in the coming kingdom of God. In the beginning a passionate hope kept the line taut between their present experience and God's future, but as the days wore on and the suffering became intense, and the living memories of Jesus faded, and the world rolled on as before, the tension in the line slackened. The apostle Paul once captured the vibrant anticipation of those early days when he said, "The appointed time has grown very short." But, as one New Testament scholar observed, gradually the time grew "very long."

It was not despite this, but, to the contrary, *because* of this that the church preserved and repeated the urgency of Jesus' warning, "Take heed, watch; for you do not know when the time will come" (Mark 13:33). No one warns the night watchman to "stay awake!" unless he appears to be getting drowsy. Just so, the church kept Jesus' call to watchfulness alive in their memory and in their

11

worship, not because they had no problem with hope, but precisely because they *did* have difficulty hoping.

But even a warning from the lips of Jesus cannot keep us vigilant, expectant, and hopeful forever. To be blunt, we cannot "take heed and watch," no matter who told us to do it, when nothing ever happens. The writer of Mark undoubtedly knew this, and that is why, when he wrote these words, he recorded two other words of Jesus as well.

The first is simply this: "Of that day or that hour no one knows, not even the angels in heaven, nor the Son, but only the Father" (Mark 13:32). What this means, starkly put, is that God's future will not arrive when we want it, plan it, or even think we need it. It will come, not according to our timetable, but in its own good time, in God's own good time. The coming kingdom is a promise, and, Hal Lindsey's *The Late Great Planet Earth* notwithstanding, it cannot be turned into a set of predictions, which we can then manipulate. The coming kingdom is a promise from God, and it cannot be domesticated into a political agenda or reduced to the doctrine of progress. God does not provide happy endings for the futures we are engineering. God provides a future beyond our knowledge and control, and not even the angels in heaven know the hour of its coming.

But even with this caution against wanting to know too much, we are still left with too little. We still have the question of how to hope in the meantime, when nothing ever happens. And that is why the writer of Mark remembered the other word which Jesus said. This word was a story, a parable actually, about a man who went on a trip and left his servants to manage the house while he was gone. That, of course, is a description of the situation of the church, left in charge of the house while the Master is absent. What Jesus said about the servants is true also of the church: They need constantly to be on the lookout. The house can never be in disarray, because, as Jesus stated it, "You do not know when the master of the house will come, in the evening, or at midnight, or at cockcrow, or in the morning — lest he come suddenly and find you asleep" (Mark 13:35-36).

Now, at first glance, Jesus seems merely to be saying again, in story form, "Of that day or hour no one knows," but the author of

Mark hears something different, something more, in this word. The master could come "in the evening," and, in the very next chapter, he tells us that "when it was evening" Jesus ate his last meal with the disciples, and tells them, "One of you will betray me."

Or the master could come "at midnight," and Mark records that, later that night, the disciples went with Jesus to Gethsemane. While Jesus prayed his cry of anguish, the disciples, no doubt weary of waiting, slept. "Could you not watch one hour?" he said to them.

Perhaps the master will come "at cockcrow," and Peter turned to the accusing maid with a curse and a denial, "I do not know this man." The cock crowed.

Maybe the coming of the master will be "in the morning," and "as soon as it was morning," Jesus was bound and led away to his trial and to his death.

What the author of Mark has heard in Jesus' story, and has woven into the fabric of his gospel, is that every moment of the passing day is already alive with the promise of God's future. As the Church strains its sight toward the horizon of the coming kingdom, it also hears the ticking of the clock on the wall, and knows that each passing minute is filled with the potential for faith or denial, decision or tragedy, hope or despair. Those who trust in the promise of God's coming kingdom are also able to see advance signs of its coming all around them. Those who believe that, in God's good time, something is about to happen, also know that, even now, something *is* happening. The passing minutes of every day are, like iron filings drawn and aligned toward an unseen magnet, already shaped by God's future and filled with its force.

"I get the feeling here, like nowhere else," mused the man in the Searchers Class, "that something is about to happen." He said, perhaps, more than he knew. We sometimes lose sight of the fact that every moment of the church's life is formed by the expectation that something is about to happen, and this *something* has to do with God's coming in power to the world. Every time Christians recite the old phrase in the creed, "He will come to judge the quick and the dead," we disclose our hope that frail human justice, the kind one can get with a good lawyer and a full checkbook, is

13

not all the justice life holds. Come, Lord Jesus. Every time some congregation creates a clothing closet or a food pantry for those in need, they do so not because they are so naive as to think that a few used garments and a shelf of soup and cereal are going to end human need. They do so because they live today in the light of God's tomorrow, when all will be clothed in garments of light and the banquet table of the kingdom will hold a feast. Come, Lord Jesus. Every time Christian people speak words of forgiveness in circumstances of bitterness, words of love in situations of hatred, they are speaking in the future present tense. That is, they are using in the present a language which the whole creation will learn to speak in God's tomorrow. Come, Lord Jesus. Every time worshippers struggle to their feet to sing, "Come Thou Long-Expected Jesus, Born To Set Thy People Free," they are praying for, expecting, something to happen, some *one* to happen. Come Lord Jesus.

Prayer, too, is grounded in the hope that something is about to happen. There is a Hasidic story about a devout man who worked in a slaughterhouse. His work required him to utter a prayer for mercy before killing each beast. Every morning he said a tearful farewell to his family before leaving for the slaughterhouse, because he was persuaded that his ritual prayer led him into great danger. He feared that, after he called upon God, God might forcefully and devastatingly come to him before he could finish the prayer with, "Have mercy."[1] A harsh truth, but a truth nonetheless. All prayer is based on the confident hope that something is about to happen.

I once taught a confirmation class to a very small group. In fact, there were only three young girls in the class. In one session, I was instructing them about the festivals and seasons of the Christian year, and when we came to the discussion of Pentecost, I asked them if they knew what Pentecost was. Since none of them knew, I proceeded to inform them that Pentecost was "when the church was sitting in a group and the Holy Spirit landed on them like tongues of fire on their heads. Then they spoke the gospel in all the languages of the world." Two of the girls took this information in stride, but the third looked astonished, her eyes wide. I looked back at her, and finally she said, "Gosh, Reverend Long, we must have been absent that Sunday." The beauty of that moment was not that she misunderstood about Pentecost, but that she understood about the Church. In her mind, there was the possibility that the event of Pentecost could have happened, even in our Sunday service. "I get the feeling here, like nowhere else, that something is about to happen." Come, Lord Jesus.

And it was the Lord, himself, who said, "What I say to you I say to all. Watch" (Mark 13:37).

---

1. A version of this story appears in Annie Dillard, *Teaching a Stone to Talk,* (New York: Harper and Row, 1982), p. 41.

What Do You Mean, "Repent"?

Mark 1:1-8

Bright Lights, Big City is Jay McInerney's searingly-witty, emotion-ripping novel of one man's perilous drift down an alcohol and white-powder-polluted stream of delayed adolescence. The young man is bright, creative, and desperately lonely. His language is marked by the kind of sarcasm which forms at the intersection of keen intelligence, comic conceit, and human desolation. (He describes a woman he meets as having a voice "like the New Jersey state anthem played through an electric razor.") Barely holding on to his low-level job at a New York City magazine, he spends most of his time playing with casual relationships in strobe-lit Manhattan bars, wandering through graffiti-scarred scenes of urban decay, and finding his personality to be unraveling at an increasing velocity.

At one point in the novel, the young man, riding an uptown subway and trailing behind him the wreckage of a marriage, a career, and possibly a life, finds himself seated next to a Talmud-reading Hasidic Jew. Watching this Hasid move his finger across the lines of Hebrew, the young man observes,

> *This man has a God and a History, a Community ... Wearing black wool all summer must seem like a small price to pay. He believes he is one of God's chosen, whereas you feel like an integer in a random series of numbers. Still, what a ... haircut.*[1]

17

A God and a History, a Community … but what a haircut. In some ways, that comes close to the reaction of contemporary people to John the Baptist, an amalgam of awesome piety and just plain weirdness. He strides into the opening scene of the Gospel of Mark, inevitably bringing with him, for the modern reader, his Hollywood-shaped image. Out of Central Casting, by way of Wardrobe, John stands there with his tumbleweed hairdo, animal skins draped over his out-sized frame, popping honey-dipped locusts as his rough baritone howls like the desert wind to the gathering crowds, "Repent!" A God and a History, a Community … but what a haircut!

There is a truth, and there is a falsehood, in this portrait of John. The truth in the image is that John *is* intended to jar the readers of Mark, to shock our sensibilities. His presence sounds a willful note of discord in the initial harmonies of the gospel narrative. John is as out of place as a dayglow orange "Ye Must Be Born Again" sign alongside a tranquil country highway.

But what is genuinely shocking about John is not his weirdness. This is the falsehood in the popular conception of him. He is intended, not to jolt them with a memory. John is not an exotic; he is a living anachronism. His vestments are not outlandish; they are the clothing of the past. John is not "Stranger in Paradise"; he is "Auld Lang Syne." To be precise, John is dressed like the old prophet Elijah, no question about it, and the moment of his appearing is as sobering in its context as would be the arrival of Thomas Jefferson, waving a copy of the Declaration of Independence, in today's Senate chamber.

So, now we know that John is not out of this world, he is simply out of sync … but so what? Simply put, if we do not understand that John represents the past, we also cannot understand what he has to say about the future. John, like Jesus who follows him, preaches a message of repentance, but "repentance" is a slippery word, a "weasel word," as someone else has phrased it. We cannot fill it with meaning for our lives until we have come to grips with this character who has stepped out of the pages of the Old Testament and into the pages of the New.

Some people, for instance, think of repentance as something which just naturally happens to people as they move along through the journey of life. We travel along the track, accelerating smoothly, our goals established, our values set, when ... wham ... we crash into the wall of some experience we cannot handle, for which our resources are inadequate. *Our* loved one dies, or *we* get rejected by the school of our choice, or *we* have a heart attack, or *we* are laid off from our work. It happens in one form or another to everyone, and such experiences call for a changing of goals, a reformulation of values, an alteration of the ways we cope with life and make our key decisions.

This is, of course, a kind of repentance, but only a mild form. It is really more like growth, or maturation, since, in most such experiences, we do not draw a new hand, but only make a few discards and rearrange the cards we have. We adjust, but do not fundamentally change. This is not the kind of repentance preached by John the Baptist.

There are others for whom repentance is a larger, more profound, and more theological version of a New Year's resolution. The old year passes to the new, and we feel the extra inches around our waists, or taste the bitter nicotine on our tongues, or think of the hurtful and spiteful things we have said to one near to us, and we repent. We toss the butter pecan ice cream into the disposal, flush the Marlboros down the commode, or stammer out a few long-overdue words of affection and affirmation.

When we repent in this fashion, what we are doing is repudiating our past, wiping the slate clean, turning over a new leaf, beginning all over again. Carl Jung was groping toward this when he wrote,

> *In the second half of life the necessity is imposed:*
>
> •*Of recognizing no longer the validity of our former ideals, but of their contraries;*
>
> •*Of perceiving the error in what previously was our conviction;*
>
> •*Of sensing the untruth in what was our truth....*[2]

In his article "Returning to Church," which appeared in the *New York Times Magazine*, novelist Dan Wakefield movingly described his own repentance, a turn from despair to faith. Wakefield portrayed a treacherous time in his life. A long-standing relationship with a woman had just dissolved. He was out of money, and had just buried, within the span of seven months, both of his parents. His work no longer satisfied him, and drugs had become an all too attractive means of escape. "I was," he wrote, "headed for the edge of a cliff." A chance conversation in a neighborhood bar with a house painter, who was looking for a place to go to mass on Christmas Eve, led to Wakefield's own attendance at a Christmas candlelight service, then to participation in other services of worship and Bible studies, and to a gradually developing devotional life.

As Wakefield's religious involvement increased, he experienced a growing freedom from his sense of drifting purposelessness and from what he called "my assortment of life-numbing addictions." He wrote:

> ... *at some point or other they felt as if they were "lifted," taken away ... The only concept I know to describe such experience is that of "grace," and the accompanying adjective "amazing" comes to mind along with it.*[3]

Christians are familiar with this, the deepest form of a certain kind of repentance, and indeed we celebrate it. "Once I was blind, but now I see," we sing. Christians rejoice in the kind of repentance which buries the rags of a soiled past in favor of the white garments of a new future. But even though this comes closer to John's message, this is not yet fully the kind of repentance which John proclaimed.

The repentance John preached is not a mid-course correction; it is more radical than that. The repentance John preached is not repudiation of the past; it is more complex than that. The repentance John preached calls for a *revising* of the past. It calls for us to look behind before we dare to move ahead. It calls for us to encounter the past we have lived through but have not fully experienced, the past we have inherited but not inhabited, before we enter a future we do not yet comprehend.

What does this mean? Consider the experience of a business executive on the verge of implementing a shrewd business plan. The scheme involved temporarily dropping prices below the level of profitability in order to starve a smaller competitor out of the market. Then, with the market to himself, prices and profits could rise. The fact that the competitor was a struggling family-owned business, not really a major factor in the market, but the sole livelihood of a family with three small children, was known to the executive. The plan was technically legal, though, and all competitors are fair game, since business, after all, is business.

Just as the arrangements were nearly in place, the executive was called back to his hometown for the funeral of a cousin. During the graveside service, as the man sat under the funeral tent which was stretched over the family plot, his eye fell on the gravestone of his grandmother, who had died when he was only a boy. Inscribed on her stone were words from the Book of Proverbs: "She opens her mouth with wisdom, and the teaching of kindness is on her tongue."

"The teaching of kindness ..." The words seemed to be written in fire as they burned in his heart. He had read them many times before on nostalgic visits to the cemetery, but now they leapt from the past into his life. He did not merely recall his grandmother; he was confronted by her memory, judged by the commitments he vaguely knew she held, but had not considered to have any claim on his life. It was a strange and disturbing experience, and he returned to his city with no will to destroy, but to seek somehow to know and live "the teaching of kindness."

The essayist and short story writer Eudora Welty wrote in *One Writer's Beginning* about the deep insight which can result when people explore memories of experiences they thought they already fully understood. "Connections slowly emerge ... cause and effect begin to align themselves ... And suddenly a light is thrown back, as when your train rounds a curve, showing there has been a mountain of meaning rising behind you on the way you've come, is rising there still ...."[4]

A mountain of meaning rises behind you ... rising there still. *That* is the soil of the repentance John preached. John wears the clothing of an old prophet, *embodies* the history of God's people, in order to proclaim that all that God has done before, which we did not fully see, all that God has said in our memory, which we did not fully believe, has pointed to this moment, to the coming of the Messiah.

What does this repentance look like in our lives?

•Whenever we return to an old and well-worn passage in the Bible and do not, through nostalgia or willfulness, force it to say only what we expect it to say, but allow it to encounter us anew, creating new and demanding possibilities for our lives, we have repented.

•When we invoke some experience in our memory and discover, in our remembering, more evidence of the hand of God there than we first saw, more signs of the grace of God than we ever knew were there before, more call for gratitude to God than we have yet expressed, and we find in ourselves a will to live a different, more faithful and obedient tomorrow because of what we have discerned, we have repented.

•Whenever we return to the faith we have been given, to the gospel we have heard so often, to the stories which have been told again and again, and find there not a retreat, but a renewal. Whenever we discover that all that God has done in our common yesterdays is pointing us anew to the Christ who comes this day, to forgive our sins and to make possible a tomorrow of faith and joy, we have repented.

---

1. Jay McInerney, *Bright Lights, Big City* (New York: Vintage Books, 1984), p. 57.

2. Carl Jung, as quoted in Bernard Martin, *If God Does Not Die* (Richmond, Virginia: John Knox Press, 1966), p 9.

3. Dan Wakefield, "Returning to Church," *The New York Times Magazine* (December 22, 1985), p. 26.

4. Eudora Welty, *One Writer's Beginnings* (Cambridge, Massachusetts: Harvard University Press, 1984), p. 90.

There's A Man Going Around Taking Names

John 1:6-8, 19-28

There is an old black gospel song from the American South, most often sung to the driving beat of a blues guitar, which includes the following lyrics:

> *There's a man going around taking names.*
> *There's a man going around taking names.*
> *He took my father's name,*
> *And he left my heart in pain.*
> *There's a man going around taking names.*
>
> *There's a man going around taking names.*
> *There's a man going around taking names.*
> *He took my mother's name,*
> *And he left my heart in pain.*
> *There's a man going around taking names.*
>
> *There's a man going around taking names.*
> *There's a man going around taking names.*
> *He took my sister's name,*
> *And he left my heart in pain.*
> *There's a man going around taking names.*[1]

In the song, the "man going around taking names" is a metaphor, of course, for all that menaces human relationships and life — most prominently, the slave trader and, finally, death itself. And it is a fascinating image for potential evil, this idea of "taking names." Even school children can identify with it. "Now, children," warns the teacher. "I'm going to the office for a few minutes, and I'm appointing Frances to be the monitor. Don't misbehave or she will write down your name, and you'll have to deal with me when I get back." ... There's somebody around here taking names.

When John the Baptist was at work in Bethany, beyond the Jordan River, a delegation of religious officials showed up from Jerusalem. They were not there, by the way, on a package tour of the Holy Land; they were there taking names. You could tell that from the very first words to come from their mouths. "Who are you?" they said. No small talk. No pictures of grandchildren passed around. Just, "Who are you?" ... There are some people going around taking names.

There is a difference, of course, between name-seeking and name-taking. Name-seeking is usually gentle, an innocent desire to know another person. The sales rep you have just met at the convention leans over to squint at your "Hello! I'm _____" badge. The woman who has just moved into the apartment next door meets you at the mail box, extends her hand saying, "I'm Jane Morris in 4-B," and arches an eyebrow expectantly, hoping for your name in return. This is name-seeking.

Name-taking, however, does not want to *know* another person; it wants to put the other person *on trial*. "Let me see your license," says the motorcycle cop, and we respond, "Yes, officer, have I done something wrong?" We sense we are already on trial. "I'm sorry," says the clerk, "I can't take your check without proper I.D." And so we pull out the credit cards and the photo identification as if to say, "See, these will testify in the court of respectability to my good character."

Name-taking places a person on trial, puts a person under threat of judgment, and, naturally, makes us wary. Bill collectors roaming through poor, but tightly-knit, neighborhoods often discover that folks somehow cannot recall their neighbors' names, even though they have lived next door to them for thirty years. Or again, I was once the relatively innocent victim of a traffic mishap. A young man, deciding at the last minute to turn into a service station, steered too sharply and creased the fender of my car. Half a dozen people watched the accident happen, but when I approached each of them, seeking an independent witness, they were suddenly struck by a strange combination of blindness and amnesia. They had seen nothing, could not even call up the memory of their own names. Name-taking puts a person on trial, drags them unwillingly into court ... There's a man going around taking names.

"Who are you?" said the officials from Jerusalem, taking names, and quickly John moved from being a minister at work to being a man under a threat. In fact, John was now on trial. The emissaries from Jerusalem had come as judge, jury, and prosecution to put John's ministry to the test, and John was being called to the stand as the only witness for his own defense. The People of Jerusalem versus John the Baptist. Will the witness please state his name? Who are you? ... There's a man around here taking names.

But it is right at this point in the story that something very strange happens. The closest parallel to it I know about occurred in one of Woody Allen's antic movies. The scene in the movie is a courtroom, and a trial is underway. A somber judge is presiding; the jury is listening intently; the prosecuting attorney is laying out the case. Suddenly the rear doors of the courtroom swing open and a frantic, emotionally-distressed man enters. He looks wildly around, and then blurts out a tearful confession, admitting to the astonished court that he, and not the defendant, is the guilty party. A dramatic and startled silence fills the room. The only problem is that the crime to which he has confessed has nothing to do with the case being tried in that court. Slowly a puzzled look gathers on the guilty man's face. Looking anxiously at the judge, he names a particular case and asks if this is the correct court, "Next courtroom," responds the judge, pointing to the exit, and the man bolts out the door.

Just so, as soon as John had been placed under interrogation, he blurted out a confession, but, strangely enough, it was a confession which belonged in another courtroom, was pertinent to another trial: "He confessed, he did not deny, but confessed, 'I am not the Christ'" (John 1:20). The authorities had come for an affidavit about John: John provides a testimony about the Christ. There

27

are two trials going on here. The officials are conducting one, but John insists upon being a witness in the other. They attempt to put John to the test, but, ironically, his testimony turns the tables and places them on trial. Indeed, if we listen to the court record, we can ear the overlap of the two proceedings, feel the mounting frustration of the prosecutors as their key witness gives his deposition in a case they did not even know was being tried:

Prosecution: What, then? Are you Elijah?

John: I am not.

Prosecution: Are you the prophet?

John: No.

Prosecution: Who are you, then? Tell us about *yourself.* Answer the court.

John: I can speak about myself only by speaking of someone else. I cry in the wilderness, announcing the coming of another.

[The prosecution asks for a brief recess to confer. The interrogation then resumes.]

Prosecution: That is confusing. Why, then, are you baptizing?

John: I baptize with water, but there is one standing in this court at this very moment, and you do not know him. I am not worthy to untie his sandals.

Back and forth it went, the questions and the answers, the authorities conducting one trial, John giving his witness in another, until finally we are left to wonder which trial is real. Is John the defendant, or the officials? Is John on trial, or is it the world?

The earliest Christians must have heard this story of John's interrogation with great enthusiasm, and perhaps even a measure of joyous laughter. They heard it as a story about the day they put old John the Baptist on trial, and he stood up and gave his witness to Jesus in a greater courtroom, one in which his accusers had no power. They also remembered the day they tried to take Jesus' name, the day they brought Jesus himself into court, and how he, too, turned the tables and put the accuser on the stand:

> "Are you the King of the Jews?" said Pilate.
>
> "Do you say this ...?" responded Jesus, turning his accuser into the defendant.
>
> "Me? Am I a Jew? ... What have you done?"
>
> "I bear witness to the truth. Everyone who is of the truth hears my voice."
>
> "What is truth?" asked Pilate, convicting himself.

In his provocative book *Liturgies and Trials,* Richard K. Fenn has commented that "the question of whether it is God or Caesar who is on trial is at the heart of the biblical tradition ...."[2] Christians are persuaded that it is the world which is finally on trial, and they give their testimony accordingly. Placing their trust in the Christ who "will come to judge the quick and the dead," the Christian community has been bold to face all worldly accusers, whether they come from Rome with swords, from Birmingham with police dogs, from Warsaw with a rifle, from Hollywood with a sneer, or from Washington with a court order. As the folk hymn puts it, "All my trials, Lord, soon be over."

Fenn has also observed that contemporary life is a constant experience of being placed in the box and put on trial. Students in school must produce their papers, grades, and SAT scores "for the record." In a career, one is always having to demonstrate competence and justify actions. A stockholders' meeting places the achievements of the corporate officers on trial. Single people and divorced people are often accused in the court of gossip of being unable to maintain long-term relationships. Parents enroll in "effectiveness training" seminars, lest they be found guilty of inadequate methods of raising their children. And now that dozens of paperback books have mapped the dark regions of the unconscious, there is opened up, according to Fenn, "a source of accusations or of offensive motives that turns a lifetime into a perpetual trial with fresh evidence continually arising from buried sources."[3] ... There's always somebody going around taking names.

We are under constant trial, and it is no wonder, then, that one of the ways Christians have always understood the good news of what has happened in Jesus Christ is in terms of already being acquitted in the highest court of all. The apostle Paul once asked, "Who shall bring any charge against God's elect? ... Who is to condemn?" The answer: No one, because the Judge himself was the very one who died for us, was raised from the dead, and even now prays for us (Romans 8:34).

The world places us on trial every day, but what the world does not know is that we have already been tried in a greater court and, through the mercy of Christ, we have been found "not guilty." Like John, the Christian community knows that there are two trials going on. The accusations and condemnations of the world are painful, but they finally have no lasting power, because our case has been pled before another judge in whom there is no condemnation. "There stands among you," said John to his accusers, "one whom you do not know," and when, the next day, John saw Jesus himself, he continued his testimony in the trial which really matters, "Behold the Lamb of God, who takes away the sin of the world!" The accusers of the world try to take our names, but in Jesus Christ we have been given a new name, and the world cannot ever take it.

> *There stands a tree in paradise,*
> *and the pilgrims call it "The Tree of Life";*
> *All my trials, Lord, soon be over.*

In the television series *Roots* there is a scene in which the slave traders are trying to break the spirit of the young black man named

Kunta Kinte, whom they have captured and brought to America from his African homeland. They have tied him to a tree, and with whips they are attempting to beat into him a new and submissive identity, "Your name is Toby," they say. The young man resists, and the whips fall. "Your name is Toby." More resistance, and the whips fall again and again. Finally the punishment is too severe, and the young man hangs his head in defeat and speaks his slave name, "Toby."

I once heard a black minister speak of his own enraged reaction when he saw that episode. He admitted that, for a moment, he was consumed with hatred, not only for those who were beating Kunta Kinte, but for all white people, for all who, through the whip of racism, bring humiliation and shame to others. The only thing that kept this hatred from settling into his heart, he said, was the deep awareness of his faith in another man, a man who was also tied to a tree and beaten. "They took this man's life," he said, "but they never took his name. And one day every knee will bow and every tongue will confess that name. Jesus is Lord."

---

1. "There's a Man Going Around Taking Names," from *Religious Music: Solo and Performance* (Album number in The Library of Congress "Folk Music in America" series, 1978). Words in the public domain.

2. Richard K. Fenn, *Liturgies and Trials: The Secularization of Religious Language* (New York: The Pilgrim Press, 1982), p. 49.

3. *Ibid.*, p. 27.

Where's
The Treasure?

Luke 1:26-38

When I was a child there was a game we would play in our neighborhood to pass the time on rainy afternoons. It was a game of the imagination, and if it had a name, which I don't think it did, it would have been called "Where Would You Leave the Treasure?" The idea was this: Suppose you had a large amount of money, a treasure really, but some unexpected crisis has come up, and suddenly you have to leave the treasure with someone for safekeeping. You can't put it in the bank or bury it under the oak tree in the back yard — there isn't time. The rule of the game is that you have to *entrust* it to someone, some human being. Whom would you choose? The fun of the game, of course, was sitting around in a circle and exploring all the character flaws and virtues of the various possibilities, searching for a trustworthy person.

"How about the school principal?" someone would suggest.

"Nah, he'd probably steal it."

"Well, how about the preacher?"

"Too risky. He'd probably put it in the collection plate."

"Okay, then, what about your sister?"

"Are you kidding? She'd want to split it."

And on it would go, the search for just the right person to keep the treasure. In the mind of a child, the stakes were high: your whole treasure risked on something as fragile as the trustworthiness of another human being.

Now, one way to read the first chapter of the Gospel of Luke is a divine version of "Where Would You Leave the Treasure?" God was searching for some place in human life to leave the treasure. In God's case, the treasure was not gold, but the gospel. The treasure was not silver, but news ... good news. Not cold, hard cash, but the deep, rich, and abiding promise that, when all is said and done, we are not alone, that God is finally "God with us," at work in our world, setting things right. That's the treasure. Despite appearances to the contrary, there is coming a time when swords will be beaten into plowshares, and peace will flow like a river. That's the treasure. The day is coming when justice will cover the earth like the sea, and empty barns, and empty stomachs, and empty hearts will be filled with grain and honey, joy and hope, and the dark stain of human destruction will be bleached clean by the grace of God. That's the treasure.

Now, where in the world do you leave a treasure like that? More fragile than silver, in a way, and yet infinitely more valuable. A treasure able to be squandered, dismissed, rationalized, even crucified. Where do you leave a treasure like that so that it will be preserved, cherished, and allowed to grow?

That's what Luke wants to tell us. Luke wants to tell us the story of where God decided to leave the treasure, and this is the way he begins: "In the days of Herod, king of Judea ..." (Luke 1:5), almost as if to say, "Now there's a possibility!" God could have left the treasure with the Herods of the world, with the politicians, the ones who pave the roads and collect the taxes, the ones who build the schools and pass the laws, the ones who command the armies and provide for the care of the weak. God could have left the treasure with the Herods, and it's not as strange a possibility as it might at first seen, because after all, the treasure is in part *political*. The treasure is the news that God is at work in the world to pull tyrants off their high horses and to lift up those who hunger and thirst for justice. That when one more starving child in Africa — or anywhere else — dies, something at the heart of God dies, too. That God is at work to break the deadlocks, to fill the bowls with food, and to send the greedy away empty. That every valley shall be exalted and every mountain and hill made low — and that's not real estate; that's politics!

And since it is politics, it would have made a certain kind of sense for God to have entrusted the treasure to the movers and the shakers — the Herods of the world.

But God did not leave the treasure with Herod, because the gospel is the good news that, if there is to be justice in the world, there can only be one true King. If there is peace in the world, there can only be one true Ruler. If there is to be mercy, there can only be one true Lord ... and his name is not Herod.

Every year at the Metropolitan Museum of Art in New York, there is displayed, beneath the great Christmas tree, a beautiful eighteenth century Neapolitan nativity scene. In many ways it is a very familiar scene. The usual characters are all there: shepherds roused from sleep by the voices of angels; the exotic wisemen from the East seeking, as Auden once put it, "how to be human now"; Joseph; Mary; the babe — all are there, each figure an artistic marvel of wood, clay, and paint. There is, however, something surprising about this scene, something unexpected here, easily missed by the causal observer. What is strange here is that the stable, and the shepherds, and the cradle are set, not in the expected small town of Bethlehem, but among the ruins of mighty Roman columns. The fragile manger is surrounded by broken and decaying columns. The artists knew the meaning of the treasure: The gospel, the birth of God's new age, was also the death of the old world.[1]

Herods know in their souls what we perhaps have passed over too lightly: God's presence in the world means finally the end of their own power. They seek not to preserve the treasure, but to crush it. For Herod, the gospel is news too bad to be endured, and Luke wants us to see that God had to find another place to leave the treasure.

"In the days of Herod ... there was a priest named Zechariah ..." (Luke 1:5), Luke tells us, and there's another possibility. God could have left the treasure with the Zechariahs of the world, the ones who think holy thoughts, handle holy things, and perform holy deeds. God could have left the treasure with the Zechariahs, and it's not a strange thought, because Zechariah is a priest. Priests are theologians of a sort, and, after all, the treasure is, in part, *theological.* The treasure is the good news that it is *God* who is at work to set things right, that it is *God* who gathers up all efforts of human good will and gives them strength beyond their measure, mercy beyond their depth, and hope beyond their grandest dreams. It is *God* who has made us, and *God* who is with us, and *God* who reclaims us, and not we ourselves. So, Zechariah, a man who handles holy things, and thinks holy thoughts, and performs holy deeds, would be a good place to leave the treasure.

There are signs that God did indeed consider leaving the treasure with his priest Zechariah. Zechariah was an ordinary priest, with the ordinary priestly responsibilities of burning incense and making sacrifices up at the Temple, and he had done the ordinary thing of marrying Elizabeth, herself the daughter of a priest. But he and Elizabeth had one very extraordinary problem. They had no children — could have no children — for Elizabeth was barren, and for reasons which have to do with the culture of the first century, that was a pain to them both and an embarrassment to Elizabeth. Then, one day in the Temple, when Zechariah was lighting the incense, God — almost as a way of testing to see if Zechariah were a good place to leave the treasure — gave Zechariah a taste of the good news, an anticipatory touch of the treasure. An angel appeared to Zechariah and told him, "Do not be afraid, your prayer has been answered. You will have great joy and gladness. Your wife will become pregnant and bear a son."

It was then that Zechariah, who thought holy thoughts, and handled holy things, and performed holy deeds, showed that he was not the place to leave the treasure. Zechariah, so familiar with the holy, finally could not believe the presence of the holy when it intruded into his life. "How shall I know this?" he whined. "I need proof. I'm an old man. This is impossible. My wife is an old woman. How shall I know this? I need proof."

And in a scene of great sadness, the angel reaches forth toward Zechariah's lips, saying, "You will be silent. You will be unable to speak, for you did not believe my words." There is a familiarity with the holy which, ironically, produces a numbness to the holy, and Zechariah was not the place to leave the treasure. For Herod, the gospel was news too bad to be endured. For Zechariah, it was too amazing to be believed, too good to be true.

There is a well-known legend about a seminary student approaching the great theologian Paul Tillich. Tillich had just lectured on the authority of the Scripture, and the student was clutching in his hand a large, black, leather-bound Bible. "Do you believe this is the Word of God?" shouted the student.

Tillich looked at the student's fingers tightly gripping the book. "Not if you think you can grasp it," said Tillich. "Only when the Bible grasps you." There is an over-familiarity with things holy, which, ironically, can make us numb to the intrusion of the holy in our lives.

The novelist and essayist Annie Dillard has written about this kind of over-familiarity with the holy. She says that she does not find Christians, outside of those who worshiped in the catacombs, "sufficiently sensible of conditions." She thinks of church people in worship as children who think they are playing around with a chemistry set, but who are actually mixing up a batch of TNT. She maintains:

> *It is madness to wear ladies' straw hats and velvet hats*
> *to worship; we should all be wearing crash helmets.*
> *Ushers should issue life preservers and signal flares; they*
> *should lash us to our pews.*[2]

God did not leave the treasure with the Herods; they would crush it. God did not leave the treasure with the Zechariahs; they could not believe it. God did not leave the treasure in the courthouse or in the sanctuary. God did not leave the treasure in the palace or under the altar. It is now that Luke tells us the surprise: God left the treasure in a place which was in that time the weakest of all places, the least likely of all spots — the womb of a woman. And Luke also tells us that the first time that the gospel is proclaimed by human lips, it is not in the Roman Senate or in the Holy of Holies; it is not by Caesar, or Peter, or Paul. It is in a place the world would count for nothing: a conversation between two women, Mary and Elizabeth, facing their pregnancies. God left the treasure in a woman's womb, and it is in a conversation about stretch marks and swollen ankles that the treasure is first proclaimed.

For Herod, the news was too bad to be endured. For Zechariah it was news too amazing to be believed. But for Mary, too unimportant to be counted, it was, in Frederick Buechner's phrase, "too good not to be true."

Maybe Luke wants us to know that the treasure of the gospel, which will one day fill the earth with its power, must first be planted in those weak and helpless places which yearn for it the most, hunger for it most deeply, and thus can believe and cherish it most fully.

There is a scene in Tennessee Williams' *A Streetcar Named Desire* when Blanche, an unlovely person desperately seeking love, meets Mitch, a man who is grossly overweight, who is embarrassed that he perspires profusely, and who, like Blanche, is frantically lonely. It is not their strength, but their mutual weakness, which brings them together, and because they are both so needy, Blanche is able to trust Mitch with the tragic story of her life. Mitch then takes her in his arms and says, "You need somebody, and I need somebody, too. Could it be you and me, Blanche?"

She looks at him in amazement, then reaches for him, her eyes filling with tears, and says, "Sometimes there's God, so quickly."[3]

It is the places of weakness in our lives and in the world which are most open to the amazing intrusion of God's presence. And part of the good news is that it is precisely there where God leaves the treasure. God does not come to that part of us which swaggers through life, confident in our self-sufficiency. God, rather, leaves the treasure in the broken places where we know we cannot make it on our own. God does not come to us in that part of us which brushes aside all who threaten our status, all who bore or bother us. God comes to us in those rare moments when we transcend our own selfishness long enough to glimpse the needs of others and to feel those needs deeply enough to hunger and thirst for God to set it right. As the old hymn puts it:

> *When other helpers fail,*
> *and comforts flee,*
> *Help of the helpless,*
> *O abide with me.*[4]

38

On the wall of the museum of the concentration camp at Dachau is a moving photograph of a mother and her little girl being taken to a gas chamber at Auschwitz. The girl, who is walking in front of her mother, does not know where she is going. The mother, who walks behind, does know, but there is nothing, absolutely nothing, the mother can do to stop this tragedy. In her helplessness, she performs the only act of love left to her. She places her hand over her little girl's eyes so, at least, she will not have to see the horror which faces her. When people see this picture in the museum, they do not move quickly or easily to the next one. You can feel their emotion, almost hear their cries, "O God, don't let that be all there is. Somewhere, somehow, set things right."

Luke's word to us this day is that God hears those prayers, and that it is into just such situations of hopelessness and helplessness that the power of God is born. It is there that God entrusts the treasure, lifting up the lowly and filling the hungry with good things — setting things right.

On a dark night in a feed stall in Bethlehem, the treasure which was entrusted to Mary became the treasure for us all. All the Herods and all the priests and all the powers-that-be gathered around to do their worst. But on Easter morning, just as Mary said, "God stretched out his mighty arm …."

---

1. From Thomas G. Long, "Foreword," *Journal for Preachers,* Vol. I, No. 1 (Advent, 1981), p. 3.

2. Annie Dillard, *Teaching a Stone to Talk* (New York: Harper and Row Publishers, 1982), p. 40.

3. Tennessee Williams, "A Streetcar Named Desire," as quoted in Sharon Blessum Sawatzky, "Sometimes There's God So Quickly," *Spinning a Sacred Yarn* (New York: Pilgrim Press, 1981), p. 188.

4. Henry F. Lyte, "Abide With Me: Fast Falls the Eventide." Words in the public domain.

Shepherds
And Bathrobes

Luke 2:8-20

Sometimes the events described in the Bible bowl us over with their sheer size. The picture in Genesis of God commanding light and darkness to go their separate ways, summoning the seven seas like charters, and, with a word, drawing up the massive continents from the primordial ooze of the formless earth. That's scale! Or, hundreds of thundering Egyptian chariots dashing headlong after fleeing Hebrew slaves. Suddenly the once dry gap in the sea is invaded by a violent wall of water, foam filling the nostrils of horses, their eyes white with fear. Horsemen are thrown from their mounts. Charioteers are swept away by the swirling torrent. Then a death-marked stillness settles on the surface of the sea. Immense! Or again, the vision in the Book of Revelation of the saints in heaven gathered in a multitude greater than the eye can see, an ocean of faces and white robes larger than the mind can measure, an endless throng finding the place in their hymn books, and triumphantly singing, "Hallelujah! Salvation and glory and power belong to our God!" Compared to this, the Mormon Tabernacle Choir sounds like a quartet.

In the face of scenes of such magnitude, the church's attempts to make them come alive in worship have seemed like a frail and tiny vessel, a thimble dipped into the ocean. How do mere sermons and hymns, prayers and readings, anthems and responses encompass events of such breadth and height? William Sloane Coffin, the pastor of New York City's Riverside Church, once told of the Easter sunrise service held annually on the rim of the Grand

Canyon. As the resurrection account was read about the angel rolling away the stone from the tomb, a massive bounder was pushed over the edge and the congregation watched it crash mightily into the depths of the canyon. "Too dramatic?" asks Coffin. "No," he replies, "the Gospel message itself demands such drama."[2]

Tonight is Christmas Eve, and the familiar story we have heard from Luke's gospel is itself one of those events which threatens to overwhelm us by its scope. It begins, to be sure, in a small and gentle way, shepherds resting on a Judean hillside keeping wary watch over the flocks. But suddenly the episode spills beyond the edges of imagination's canvas. The night sky is flooded by the light of glory. First there is one angel, then another and another, until finally there is a heavenly host, putting on an angelic display so terrifyingly spectacular that the King James Bible seems deeply understated when it reports that the shepherds "were sore afraid."

Tonight, all across the land, in fellowship halls, sanctuaries, and church basements, those who know and love this story will try to re-create it, and the results, compared to the original, will seem pitiably small. A gaggle of neighborhood boys, the very ones we have seen kicking a soccer ball across the front yard, will stand on a hillside of indoor-outdoor carpet, guarding cardboard and cotton-ball sheep with makeshift staffs, their terry-cloth bathrobes almost, but not quite, hiding their worn Adidas sneakers. Suddenly a gauzily angelic version of the little girl from next door will burst onto the scene, lisping the good news through the gap where her next tooth will eventually grow. Other angels will soon join her, their foil-wrapped wings bouncing wildly to the beat of "Gloria in Excelsis." When the angels have fluttered to stage right, the shepherds will lumber left to Bethlehem to find a fawn-eyed Mary and a sheepish Joseph, whose steady downward gaze is fixed upon the blanket-wrapped doll in the plywood creche.

These bathrobe Christmas pageants, and indeed *all* of our attempts to convey the range and power of whatever-in-the name-of-God happened that night to those shepherds, seem so weak and small. They appear to dim the blinding luminosity of those moments to the flicker of a single candle, to reduce the size of those great events to the scale of a Hallmark Christmas card. As the essayist Annie Dillard once put it,

> ... *if you send any shepherds a Christmas card on which is printed a three-by-three photograph of the angel of the Lord, the glory of the Lord, and a multitude of the heavenly host, they will not be sore afraid.*[3]

Perhaps this is so, but before we put the bathrobes back into the closet and dismantle the plywood crib, we should look again and carefully at the way in which Luke describes this event. The important thing to notice is that Luke does not dazzle us with spacious description. How bright was this shining glory of the Lord? Luke does not say. What did the angels look like? Luke is silent. How many were there? Luke declines to count them. What exactly were the angels doing as they filled the sky with song? Luke has no comment. What expression was on the face of the newborn savior? Luke says nothing. It is as if Luke pulls our attention away from the events themselves and focuses it instead on something else, namely the *responses* of those who were involved. The shepherds were "sore afraid," but returned from Bethlehem "glorifying and praising God for all they had heard and seen." The people who heard their reports "wondered at what the shepherds had told them." Mary "kept all these things, pondering them in her heart." As for the "glory of the Lord," Luke is reticent, but when it comes to those upon whom it shone, he breaks his descriptive silence and saves his fullest language to portray what happened in their lives and hearts.

Frederick Buechner tells in one of his sermons about some useful advice he once received from a young ship's officer aboard a British freighter. It was night; the ship was in the middle of the Atlantic Ocean, and the officer had been peering into the darkness, looking for the lights of the other ships. He told Buechner that the way to see lights on the horizon is not to look straight at the horizon, but to look just above the horizon. You can see the lights better, he told Buechner, when you do not try to look at them *directly*. "Since then," writes Buechner, "I have learned that it is also the way to see other things."[4]

Just so, Luke moves our gaze from the light on the horizon to the places just above, below, and off to one side. We are told of the light which filled the world that night, but we do not really *see* it. We see instead the reflection of that light on the faces and in the hearts of those who were present.

Surely one of the reasons Luke does this is because he knew how arrogant it would be to attempt to do otherwise. What pushed back the darkness that night was nothing less than the glory of God, and human language and action simply cannot scale those heights. To try to do so risks vanity at best, idolatry at worst. I once attended the annual Christmas show at New York's Radio City Music Hall, and an impressive show it was. After entertaining presentations of seasonal chestnuts, like Dickens' "A Christmas Carol," the review moved to its finale, a re-creation of the nativity itself. In command of a stage the size of a city block and with the virtually unlimited resources of Broadway at their disposal, the producers were not at all reluctant to attempt to give us a taste of the real thing. There were no neighborhood kids wandering uneasily around the sets here. These shepherds were professional actors in authentic garb. Real sheep and camels made their way to center stage, where a matinee-idol Joseph and a Mary of breathtaking beauty cuddled a live, irresistibly precious, baby Jesus. Above the scene was a flashing, electric star, several stories high, surrounded by fluttering angels projected almost magically from a booth in the rear. Handel's "Hallelujah Chorus" filled the theater with several hundred decibels of bone-vibrating sound. The place jumped with light and movement, and the audience scarcely knew where to look. It was a massive spectacle, which lacked only one thing — the glory of the Lord. The very attempt to look directly at this moment, to replicate its majestic size, had, ironically, drained it of all mystery. Everyone's eyes were filled, but no one pondered anything in her heart.

But there is another, and more important, reason why Luke turns our gaze from the light itself toward the faces of those people who were illumined by it. Luke wants us to search those faces and to find our *own* faces reflected there, to find *ourselves* once again filled with wonder, to ponder these things in *our* hearts, to contemplate the possibility that *we*, too, might glorify and praise God this Christmas Eve for all that we have experienced because of the life of the Christ child born that night. As New Testament scholar Raymond Brown stated it, the shepherds "are the forerunners ... of future believers who will glorify God for what they have heard and will praise God for what they have seen."[5] Luke does not want us to be fascinated by this story's height; he invites us instead to explore for ourselves its depth.

There was once a Christmas pageant at a small church in which the part of the innkeeper at Bethlehem was played by a high school student. He was a quiet and polite boy, but the kind of boy for whom the word "awkward" was an apt description — awkward in manner, awkward in social relationships, even awkward in size, his growing frame always pushing at the limits of his clothing. His peers liked him well enough, but he was the sort of person who was easy to overlook, to exclude from the center of things. When Joseph and Mary appeared at the inn, he stood ... awkwardly ... in the doorway, slumping a bit toward the couple as they made their request for lodging. He then dutifully recited his one line, "There is no room in the inn." But as Mary and Joseph turned and walked wearily away toward the cattle stall where they would spend the night, the boy continued to watch them with eyes filled with compassion. Suddenly responding to a grace which, though not part of the script, filled the moment, he startled himself, the holy couple, and the audience, by calling, "Wait a minute. Don't go. You can have my room."

And that is why, when all is said and done, those Christmas pageants in church fellowship halls, sanctuaries, and basements perhaps capture the Christmas story best. They are, like Luke's gospel itself, pictures of what happens to unremarkable people in a dark world when suddenly, and in ways they do not fully understand, the glory of the Lord shines upon them. Like the characters in Luke, the players in these pageants do not pretend to express the light; they only try to reflect it. The cast, drawn from those who populate our workaday lives, embodies in its very ordinariness the truth of the angel's promise, "Unto *you* is born this day a Savior." There is the kid from down the street, wearing a tinfoil crown and carrying a cigar box of frankincense. There is our daughter, adjusting her wire halo as she lauds, "My soul magnifies the Lord." And there we are, too, staffs in hand, stumbling over each other to get near the newborn King, our unsteady voices searching for the correct pitch as we sing anew, "O, come, let us adore Him, O, come, let us adore Him, Christ the Lord."

----

1. Portions of this sermon previously appeared in Thomas G. Long, "Bit Parts in the Christmas Pageant," *Journal for Preachers,* Vol. VI, No. 1 (Advent, 1982), pp. 14-21. This material is used by permission.

2. William Sloane Coffin, "Our Resurrection, Too," in Paul H. Sherry (ed.), *The Riverside Preachers* (New York: The Pilgrim Press, 1978), p. 162.

3. Annie Dillard, *Teaching a Stone to Talk* (New York: Harper and Row, 1982), p. 95.

4. Frederick Buechner, "The End is Life," in *The Magnificent Defeat* (New York: The Seabury Press, 1966), pp. 79-80.

5. Raymond E. Brown, *The Birth of the Messiah* (Garden City, N.Y.: Image Books, 1977), p. 429.

They Also
Serve Who Wait

Luke 2:25-40

"The whole thing is rotten," said Morris Weiser, as he tapped his cane on the vaulted ceiling of the old and decaying synagogue in New York's lower east side. Morris Weiser was among the few Jews who survived the Janowska concentration camp in Poland, and now, a retired butcher in his seventies, his one remaining passion is to keep alive the Chasam Sopher synagogue. The synagogue has few Sabbath worshipers now, but Morris has put all of his savings into this place, sustains it by his constant effort, keeps it barely alive by the sheer force of his will. "When God saved me from Hitler," he said, "I promised that in any country I come I will do something for God."

The synagogue, like the tenements which fill the neighborhood in which it stands, is marked by peeling paint, deteriorating floors, and falling plaster. Morris, himself, is feeling the wearing effects of the passing days. "I'm broken down like this shul," he confesses.

In the days before the war, Morris had been a promising young medical student, but now his youth is gone, his money is gone, and all he has left are the synagogue and hope. And so, Morris Weiser does what he can, and he waits. Casting his eyes over the vacant pews, he vows that someday "there'll be a lot of Jews here."[1]

Simeon and Anna were also aging Jews who clung to their hope ... and waited. Luke tells us that Simeon and Anna lived in Jerusalem and were among those who looked expectantly for God to come in power to save his people. Like Morris, who believes

47

that a God who can save will not leave the synagogue forever empty, Simeon and Anna believed that a God who can save would not leave the chosen people forever empty. And so, like Morris, they did what they could, and they waited. New Testament scholar Raymond Brown gives us the best translation of Luke's descriptions of them: Simeon "was upright and devout, waiting for the consolation of Israel." Anna "never left the Temple courts; day and night she worshiped God, fasting and praying," for she was among "those waiting for the redemption of Israel."[2]

It is never easy to wait for anything of importance — for Christmas, for the plane carrying the one we love, for the morning to relieve the sleepless night, for the healing word in a bitter argument, for the toilsome task to be done, for the labor to be over and the child to be born, for death. It is never easy to wait.

It is hardest of all to wait for God. Not many can bear its harsh discipline. Not many can attain its delicate balance of action and hope. Not many can achieve its deep wisdom. Not many can endure its long and dark hours. Therefore, since the demands of waiting for God are so great, there is always the temptation to transform waiting for God into something else, something less.

There are some who would change waiting for God into passivity. "It is *God* for whom we wait," they say, "so nothing can be done until God comes. Nation will rage against nation, and there is nothing we can do about it. We must wait for God to bring us peace. The poor we will always have with us, and it is God who will take care of them. We live in an evil and unjust world, sad, but true, and we must wait for God to set things right."

But waiting for God is not like sitting in a darkened theater, idly waiting for the movie to begin. Waiting for God is more like waiting for an honored guest to arrive at our home. There is much work to be done; everything must be made ready. Every sweep of the broom, every pressing of the dough, every setting of the table is done in anticipation of the needs and wishes of the one who is to come.

When James Watt was Secretary of the Interior, he often infuriated environmentalists by his careless treatment of the nation's natural resources. He advocated the granting of oil leases in wilderness areas, and he worked to permit strip-mining in areas adjacent to national parks. Particularly troubling was the fact that Watt based his decisions on religious as well as political grounds. A fundamentalist Christian, Watt saw no real reason to preserve the environment, since Jesus would be coming soon. While Watt can perhaps be admired for his undeserving faith in the coming Christ, his actions demonstrated a serious misunderstanding of the Christ who is coming. The Christ for whom we wait is the very one "in whom all things were created," and a selfish lack of care for the creation is no way to wait for his coming.

In the early '60s, at the height of the civil rights movement, a group of white ministers issued a public statement urging Dr. Martin Luther King, in the name of the Christian faith, to be more patient in his quest for justice and to relax the relentless struggle for civil rights. King's response came in the form of the famous "Letter from Birmingham Jail." In the letter, King indicated that he had received similar requests for delay, indeed, that he had just gotten a letter from a "white brother in Texas" who wrote, "... It is possible you are in too great a religious hurry ... The teachings of Christ take time to come to earth." Dr. King replied that such an attitude stemmed from a sad misunderstanding of time, the notion that time itself cures all ills. Time, King argued, could be used for good or for evil. Human progress, he said, is not inevitable, but rather ...

> ... it comes through the tireless efforts of men willing to be co-workers with God, and without this hard work, time itself becomes an ally of the forces of social stagnation. We must use time creatively, in the knowledge that the time is always ripe to do right.[3]

King knew that complete justice must await the coming of God. That was the theme of his final sermon in which he proclaimed, "I've been to the mountaintop. I've seen the promised land." But he was persuaded that while we wait, "the time is always ripe to do right." Simeon and Anna were waiting for God to come, but they also were not passive in their waiting. Simeon was full of devotion and did what was just. Anna kept the lights burning at the Temple with her ceaseless worship. They waited, but, while they waited, they did what they could.

On the other hand, there are others who are weary of waiting for God, who would turn instead to more immediate and tangible sources for action and hope. According to the account in the *New York Times,* it was just before Christmas several years ago that David Storch, a music teacher, borrowed a copy of the score of Handel's *Messiah* from the Brooklyn Public Library. Through a clerical error, however, the transaction was not recorded. There were several other requests for the score, and the library staff, unaware that it had been checked out, spent many hours searching in vain for it through the stacks. On the day that Storch returned it, placing it on the circulation desk, he was astonished to hear the librarian spontaneously, joyously, and loudly shout, "The *Messiah* is here! The *Messiah* is back!" Every head in the library turned toward the voice, but, alas, as the *Times* reported, "A few minutes later everyone went back to work."[4]

A wry story, but also a parable of the often dashed expectations of those who wait for God. Someone cries, "Peace, peace," but there is no peace. Another says, "Comfort, comfort," but there is little comfort. "Come, thou long-expected Jesus," goes the prayerful hymn, and heads turn in a moment of curious interest, then, seeing nothing, go back to work. And so, weary of waiting on a God who does not come, we lower our horizons, fold our hands in prayer to more tangible gods to give us purpose, and turn to more immediate and reliable resources for hope. We build shiny sanctuaries of glass and steel where we can celebrate "possibility thinking" and the other human potentials, which we hope will save us from our self-doubt, if not our sins. We fill the silos and the skies with ever more potent weapons of destruction, which we hope will save us from each other. And we summon the elixirs of modern medicine to save us from disease, aging, and finally from death. In short, tired of waiting for the true God, we create our own.

In Arnold Schoenberg's opera, "Moses and Aaron," while Moses is on the mountaintop receiving the Law, Aaron is left in the valley to wait with the people. Exhausted, impatient, and deprived of the vision of God's presence, the people cry to Aaron, "Point God out! We want to kneel down ... But then, where is he? Point him out!" Finally Aaron yields to their plea, forging for them a god they can touch, a god for whom they never have to wait. "O Israel," he says,

> *... I return your gods to you,*
> *and also give you to them,*
> *just as you have demanded.*
> *You shall provide the stuff;*
> *I shall give it a form ....*[4]

But our gods made of positive thoughts, nuclear megatons, management objectives, secular therapies, and cosmetic skill cannot save us. Indeed they become burdens to us, heavy to carry, costly to maintain. It is God alone who saves, and part of what it means to be fully human is to wait for his coming. Jesuit priest William F. Lynch has observed that there are two kinds of waiting. One kind waits because "there is nothing else to do." The other is born out of hope. The decision to engage in this hopeful kind of waiting ...

> *... is one of the great human acts. It includes, surely, the*
> *acceptance of darkness, sometimes its defiance. It includes the enlarging of one's perspective beyond a present*
> *moment ... It simply chooses to wait, and in so doing*
> *gives the future the only chance it has to emerge.*[5]

Simeon and Anna did not wait because "there was nothing else to do," but because they had hope. Therefore their waiting was not a vacuum, devoid of activity. They worked and worshiped, performed acts of justice and prayer. While they waited, they defied the darkness by serving God, because it was for the light of *God* that they waited. They did what they could, and they waited.

And, Luke tells us, God did come to them. Who knows what they were expecting, but surely it was not this: a fragile baby bundled into the Temple by two young parents who were eager to

51

obey the ritual law of purification, but who were too poor to afford the sacrifice of a lamb and brought with them instead the acceptable substitute, a pair of birds. A man, a woman, two birds, and a baby. Can this be the heralded and hoped-for coming of God?

It is hard to wait for God. There are some who wait for God passively, and there are some who impatiently refuse to wait, but the hardest part of waiting for God is to recognize and accept God when he comes and how he comes. We pray for God to come and give us young people to fill the pews, and God comes, not bringing more people but a new and demanding mission. We pray for God to give us inner peace, and God comes to us bringing another struggle. We pray for God to come and heal, and God comes to us at graveside saying, "I am the Resurrection and the Life." We pray for God to come and console his people, and in the front door of the Temple walk two new and uncertain parents carrying a pair of birds ... and a baby who will die on a cross.

But old Anna looked, and somehow she knew that she had seen the fulfillment of her hope and Israel's hope. Old Simeon looked, and he knew, too. He knew that God indeed had come, and he also knew that this coming of God, like all of God's comings, both met human need and defied human expectation, that it would bring both salvation and demand, great hope and great cost. As soon as he had said, "Mine eyes have seen thy salvation," he added the warning, "This child is set for the fall and rising of many in Israel." Every coming of God meets our needs, but also violates our expectations and demands our lives.

When the master artist Giotto expressed this story in paint, he, too, saw the fulfillment and the demand, the joy and the hope, in the coming of God. His "Presentation in the Temple" is, according to art critic John W. Dixon, Jr., "one of the few genuinely witty paintings in great art."[6] Simeon holds the baby Jesus, his lips moving now beneath his hoary beard, carefully reciting his oft-rehearsed lines, *"Nunc dimittis* ... Now lettest thou thy servant depart in peace." Giotto knows his Simeon. He also knows his babies, for the infant Jesus, far from resting contentedly through this aria, is responding as all babies do when held by eccentric strangers. His dark eyes are narrowed and fixed in frozen alarm on Simeon. He reaches desperately for his mother, every muscle arched away from the strange old man. Giotto knows his babies. He also knows the deep truth of this moment, for as Jesus reaches away from Simeon toward Mary, we observe that the child is suspended above the temple altar.[7] "This very human baby," observes Dixon, "is from the beginning, the eternal sacrifice for the redemption of mankind."[8]

Redemption and sacrifice. Hope and demand. So it is with the coming of God. But God will come. The God who came to Simeon and Anna will come to us, too, violating our expectations even as he comes to meet our deepest needs. Until He comes, like Anna and Simeon, we do what we can ... and wait.

---

1. Joseph Berger, "A Man Battles to Save Cherished Synagogue," *The New York Times* (July 21, 1986), section B, p. 3.

2. Raymond E. Brown, *The Birth of the Messiah* (Garden City, New York: Doubleday and Company, 1977), pp. 435-6.

3. Martin Luther King, Jr., "Letter from Birmingham Jail," in *Why We Can't Wait* (New York: Harper and Row, 1964), p. 89.

4. Arnold Schoenberg, "Moses and Aaron," as translated in Karl H. Worner, *Schoenberg's "Moses and Aaron"* (London: Faber and Faber, 1959), pp. 137 & 163.

5. William F. Lynch, S.J., *Images of Hope* (Baltimore: Helicon, 1967), pp. 177-8.

6. John W. Dixon, Jr., *Art and the Theological Imagination* (New York: Seabury Press, 1978), p. 96.

7. Some of this material previously appeared in Thomas G. Long, "Bit Parts in the Christmas Pageant," *Journal for Preachers,* Vol. VI, No. 1 (Advent, 1982), p. 20. It is used by permission.

8. Dixon, p. 96.

We Interrupt
This Service

John 1:1-18

It was question and answer time at the worship workshop. I had been speaking on the theme of worship all morning to a group of people gathered in a church fellowship hall in a suburban neighborhood in Indiana. Dressed in sweatshirts and jeans, they had given up a Saturday of golf and gardening to sip coffee and listen politely as I rambled through discussions of Vatican II, Calvin's view of the Lord's Supper, the pros and cons of children's sermons, the development of the lectionary, the meanings of baptism, and other assorted topics about worship. Now, the lecturing done, I gulped down a little coffee of my own and asked if there were any questions.

A hand shot into the air. It belonged to a fiftyish man with plump cheeks and rimless glasses who was, judging by the way his hand waved and bobbed, eager to speak. "There's one thing about our worship service here which really gripes me," he complained. "To me it's like fingernails being scraped across a blackboard."

"What's that?" I cautiously asked, fully expecting him to say something about gender inclusive language, newfangled hymns, politics in the pulpit, or sermons on tithing. But it was not one of these issues which caused his aggravation.

"The announcements," he declared. "I just hate it when the minister spoils the mood of worship with all those dull announcements." Heads bobbed in vigorous agreement all around the room. The announcements were out of favor in that corner of Indiana, no question about it.

I knew what the man meant, of course. You're soaring above the pews on Sunday, your wings catching the strong breeze of the Spirit carrying you upward from "Joy to the World" toward the choir's lofty "For Unto Us a Child is Born," and then, thud ... the Christian Education Committee will meet in the library on Thursday at 7:30 ..." Like Icarus striving for the sun, you find your wax wings suddenly melting, and you plummet back to the world of flesh, dust, and committee meetings.

I know what he meant. The announcements do seem like a bag of peanuts at the opera, an ungainly moment of mundanity wedging its way into an hour of inspiration. What I tried to say to the questioner was that I understood how he felt and that, yes, the announcements were often rattled off without care or passion, and, yes, they did sometimes seem to be somewhat uninspiring, but that, after all, the details of the church's institutional life were *important,* and five minutes of them couldn't hurt, and so on..

In short, I blew it. What I should have said is that, properly understood, the announcements are one of those places where the rubber of the church's theology hits the road. Indeed, it just may be that by moving seamlessly from "Holy, Holy, Holy" to "the telephone crisis counseling ministry is in need of additional volunteers," by punctuating its soaring praise with the commas of the earthy details of its common life, the church is expressing in its worship one of its most basic convictions about the character of God: "The Word became flesh and dwelt among us ..." (John 1:14).

That affirmation about the eternal Word becoming flesh comes, of course, from the poem which opens the Gospel of John. The poem begins with violins and soaring phrases: "In the beginning was the Word, and the Word was with God, and the Word was God ..." (John 1:1). With these ethereal phrases at the beginning of John's gospel, it is no wonder that the church selected, as a symbol for John the Evangelist, the high flying eagle. If John's poem had ended after the first line, the noble Greek philosophers could have voiced their admiring approval. They, too, wanted to mount up with eagle's wings, to leave the earth behind, and to ascend into the celestial heights to be with God and his *logos*, his Word.

But John's poem does not end with the first line. The eagle suddenly dives toward the ground. The violins give way to the blunt thud of a bass drum. Heaven crashes to the earth. The closing notes of the hymn fade, and it is time for the first startlingly earthbound announcement in Christian history: "The Word became flesh and dwelt among us ...." It is here that John and the Greeks part company. The very idea that the ultimate meeting between humanity and the *logos* of God would come, not when we ascended to the airy pinnacle, but when the *logos* descended to the fleshy depths was, to employ the term of New Testament scholar Raymond Brown, "unthinkable." John's poem, Brown says, does not claim ...

> ... *that the Word entered into flesh or abided in flesh but that the Word* became *flesh. Therefore, instead of supplying the liberation from the material world that the Greek mind yearned for, the Word of God was now inextricably bound to human history.*[1]

The conviction that God refused to float in sublime isolation above time and space, but became in Jesus Christ, flesh and blood, sweat and earth, is the doctrine of the incarnation, and what it means, among other things, is that we do not escape the mundane to encounter the living God. Indeed, the announcements in worship became symbolic of the Christian truth that it is the "fleshy" details of life, the working and the serving, the community projects and the committee meetings, the being born, the marrying, and the dying, which are the arenas for our encounter with God-become-flesh in Jesus Christ. When the announcements about soup kitchens, new babies, people in the hospital, Bible studies, and meetings of Alcoholics Anonymous begin, "Holy, Holy, Holy" does not end; the church is simply confessing that *these* are the places where that holiness is to be found. "The Word became flesh ..."

Now the church has always known that affirming this doctrine of the incarnation was like carrying around a lighted stick of dynamite. On the one hand, it is capable of blasting away virtually everyone who prefers less fleshy brands of religion. For those who seek religious experience and inner peace through the inward path of meditation, for example, there is John insisting that the path of God does not end in rarified spirit, but in *flesh*. In other words, however many inward turns the path may take, it eventually leads out to the world of flesh where we are called to meet Christ in human community. One of the telling criticisms of the electronic church is that it also isolates the viewer from the "fleshiness" of human community. As one observer put it, the television church offers religious experience in the safe and sterile environment of one's own living room and not among "sniffling children, restless teenagers, hard-of-hearing grandparents, and sleepy parishioners." Moreover ...

> *When you watch television church, no one asks you to participate in a visitation program. No one challenges you to hold the attention of a junior high Sunday school class. No one asks you to take meals to shut-ins.*[2]

In short, it is all pure religion and no messy entanglements with human flesh. All of which is fine until the old eagle John swoops to earth with his announcement: "The Word became flesh ...."

On the other hand, the doctrine of incarnation blows up all naive notions of the inherent and natural holiness of life. It was God who became flesh, not flesh that became God. In the movie about Saint Francis of Assisi, *Brother Sun, Sister Moon*, the birds and all of nature preach their granola-flavored goodness to *Francis*. In the church's story, however, Francis preaches to the birds, and therein lies the crucial difference. All of creation was fallen — *all* of it. To use John's language, darkness was everywhere. In Jesus Christ, God entered creation, became flesh, and all of the darkness in the world cannot overcome the light of that saving act.

The incarnation means that, appearances to the contrary, all of human life and history is infused with holiness, but this does not mean that life is a lark or that we are called to sing as a hymn the words of the popular song, "Everything is beautiful, in its own way." Anyone who has seen the torture chambers of the Nazi regime, any surgeon who has removed a malignant tumor, any reformer who has tried to clean up government, knows that everything is *not* beautiful in its own way. To affirm the incarnation does not imply that life is rosy or that people always do the right thing or even the best they can. It does not mean that people do not waste their lives, get hurt, or hurt other people. It does not mean that there is no hardship, no drudgery, no evil, no tragedy. It would be an illusion to pretend otherwise. What it does mean is that there is no corner of experience so hidden that grace cannot find it. There is no soil so sterile that the seed of holy wonder cannot grow in it. There is no moment so dark that it can extinguish the light of God which even now shines in it. Christians do not bubble around celebrating life. They celebrate God who enters the life of creation in order to redeem it. "The Word became flesh ..."

When Christians say, "The Word became flesh and dwelt among us, full of grace and truth," they do not mean that God *is* everything, but they do mean that God is *in* everything. "In everything," wrote Paul to the Romans, "God works for good with those who love him ..." (Romans 8:28). The theologian Robert McAfee Brown likes to use in his writing the musical metaphor of themes and variations.[3] There are many musical compositions, Beethoven's Fifth Symphony for example, which begin with a clear, identifiable musical pattern, or theme. What follows in the music is a series of variations on this theme, the theme being repeated in ever more complex combinations. Sometimes the texture of these combinations is so complex that the theme is hidden, seemingly obscured by the competing and interlocking notes. But those who have heard the theme clearly stated at the beginning of the work can still make it out, can feel the music being organized by the theme. In Jesus Christ "the Word became flesh and dwelt among us, full of grace and truth ...." That's the theme of all of life heard clearly by the ears of faith, and those who have heard that distinct theme can hear it being sounded wherever the music of life is being played, no matter how jangled are the false notes surrounding it.

In her book *Pilgrim at Tinker Creek*, Annie Dillard told about seeing a mockingbird dive straight down off the roof of a four-story building. "It was an act as careless and spontaneous as the curl of a stem ..." she wrote. The mockingbird, wings held tightly against its body, descending at 32 feet per second toward the earth, spread his wings at the last possible second and floated onto the ground. Dillard said she spotted this amazing display just as she rounded a corner. No one else was there to witness it. She connected the event to the old philosophical question about the tree falling in the forest. If no one were there to hear it, goes the conundrum, would it make a sound? "The answer must be," she stated:

> ... I think, that beauty and grace are performed whether or not we will sense them. The least we can do is try to be there.[4]

Because in Jesus Christ the Word became flesh, truth and grace are at work in every place, whether or not we sense them. What we can do, of course, is to attempt to master the theme and then to try to be there wherever in life it is played anew. If we wonder where that might be, one good place to begin is by listening in worship to the announcements.

---

1. Raymond E. Brown, *The Gospel According to John (I-XII) (The Anchor Bible,* Vol. 29), (Garden City, New York: Doubleday and Company, 1966), p. 31.

2. Philip Yancey, *Open Windows* (Nashville: Thomas Nelson Publishers, 1985), p. 73.

3. See, for example, chapter eighteen in Robert McAfee Brown, *The Bible Speaks to You* (Philadelphia: The Westminster Press, 1955) , pp. 231 ff.

4. Annie Dillard, *Pilgrim at Tinker Creek,* as quoted in Yancey, p. 24.